Intercessions
in
Wors

by

Michael Vasey

Tutor of Cranmer Hall, St. John's College, Durham
Member of the Church of England Liturgical Commission

GROVE BOOKS LIMITED
Bramcote   Nottingham   NG9 3DS

CONTENTS

ACKNOWLEDGMENTS

Many thanks to friends for their prayers, to colleagues for their patience, to Tom Mendel for early morning tea in a time of crisis, to the Group for the Renewal of Worship for its encouragement, to those who sent in suggestions, to Rosalind Leech for typing the manuscript, to Colin Buchanan for his stimulus and gentle pressure, and to God, 'the source of all good desires, all right judgments and all just works'.

Michael Vasey

The quotation from *The Prayers of the Eucharist* on page 3 is reprinted by permission of Collins Liturgical Publications. That from *A New Eusebius* on page 6 is reprinted by permission of the S.P.C.K.

THE COVER PICTURE . . .

is by Peter Ashton

THIS SECOND EDITION

is virtually unchanged from the first

First Edition July 1981
Second Edition January 1988

ISSN 0144–1728
ISBN 1 85174 070 8

1. INTRODUCTION

The new communion services of the Church of England have highlighted the place of united intercessory prayer in the church's worship. In place of the long and unchanging prayer for the Church Militant of the Book of Common Prayer, Series 2 and 3 have provided a framework of biddings, prayers, and congregational responses. In many churches this has allowed great flexibility and congregational involvement. There has been place for silence and for biddings from the congregation. The prayers have often been planned by families, individuals, or parish groups. They have allowed some of the concerns and atmosphere of modern life to find a place in the Christian gathering. Rite A of ASB 1980 has taken this freedom much further giving churches not so much a framework as a do-it-yourself kit—some optional components (section 21), some alternatives (section 81), and freedom to do something else altogether (section 20). The limited freedom of series 2 and 3 has not always been successful, with the prayers led in an uncertain, repetitive, or inaudible way. The much greater freedom of Rite A is quite likely to lead to a far less satisfactory result with the loss of any clear framework for the prayer leading to less congregational involvement and even the substitution of a bland devotional ramble for any confident or specific intercessory prayer. If the freedom is to have positive results there must be skilled and well-informed leadership and greater understanding on the part of the congregation.

Although the new services have done something to brighten up the intercessions the impression given is often of a clerical monologue or of underrehearsed play acting. Rarely is there a sense that the prayer is for real, that this is the fervent, confident, expectant prayer of a congregation that acknowledges human weakness and seeks divine power. The midweek prayer meeting of many traditional evangelical parishes points to the low expectation people have of intercessory prayer in public worship. Even in churches with home groups that pray together or with meetings for praise and prayer this element often finds little expression in the main gatherings of the church.

The restoration of this element in the new communion services is not just response to need but is the conscious recovery of a well-defined and important part of the eucharistic worship of the early church.[1] Justin Martyr (c. A.D. 150) in an early description of Christian Sunday worship writes,

> 'On the day called Sun-day an assembly is held in one place of all who live in town or country, and the records of the apostles or writings of the prophets are read for as long as time allows. Then when the reader has finished the president in a discourse admonishes and exhorts us to imitate these good things. Then we all stand up together and offer prayers; and . . . when we have finished praying, bread and wine and water are brought up, and the president likewise offers prayers and thanksgivings to the best of his ability, and the people assent saying the Amen;'[2]

---

[1] R. C. D. Jasper (ed.) *The Eucharist Today* (S.P.C.K., 1974) pp.54ff.
[2] R. C. D. Jasper and G. J. Cumming (ed.), *The Prayers of the Eucharist* (Collins, 1975) p.19.

Elsewhere Justin follows his description of a baptism with an account of how the new Christian joins the brethren who 'make common prayers earnestly for ourselves and for him who has been enlightened and for all others everywhere'. The prayers were concluded with the kiss of peace. The reading of the scriptures was open to all but only baptized believers could join the church for prayer and the eucharist.[1] The *Didascalia,* a third century Church Order, lays down that Christians who are openly sinning or quarrelling shall not take part in the prayers or the eucharist until they repent and are reconciled. 'If then you keep malice against your brother, or he against you, your prayer is not heard and your eucharist is not accepted.'[2] The intercessions were a distinct element in the pattern of early Christian worship that came between the time of reading and instruction from the scriptures and the eucharist itself. The traditional posture for prayer of standing with hands outstretched and palms turned upwards emphasized the active engagement of each Christian in the prayer.

The restoring of this element of intercession in modern communion services comes partly from the discovery by liturgical scholars of this common pattern in the second and following centuries. It also reflects a desire to overcome divisions between Christian denominations by rediscovering common roots. Our situation is very different from that of the church in the third century and it is not possible for us to adopt their way of doing things wholesale. Rite A not only allows greater flexibility but will be used to celebrate the communion in very different situations such as quiet early morning services, weekly gatherings of a stable Christian community, major gatherings and festival celebrations of the church. The notion of united fervent intercessory prayer will need developing in very different ways appropriate to each situation.

[1] See also G. J. Cuming (ed.) *Hippolytus: A Text for Students* (Grove Liturgical Study 8, 1976) section 16, p.16.

[2] R. H. Connolly (ed.) *Didascalia Apostolorum* Ch. X, or Sebastian Brock and Michael Vasey (eds.) *The Liturgical Portions of The Didascalia* (Grove Liturgical Study no. 29, 1982), chap. 11, p.14; cf. also 1 Tim. 2.8.

2. BRIEF HISTORY

The New Testament

The New Testament offers us nothing as neat as the pattern of worship that already existed by the time of Justin. What stands out is that prayer together played a large part in the life of the early Christian communities. The Acts of the Apostles not only presents us with common prayer as a central activity of the post-Pentecost church (Acts 2.42) but gives us a whole string of vignettes of what this meant in practice (1.14, 2.46-7, 4.23ff., 12.12, 13.1-3, 14.23 etc.). The impression given there is fully confirmed by St. Paul's letters. References to his own prayer and the prayer of the churches are all-pervasive and show that prayer, public and private, played a more prominent and well-integrated part in the life of these churches than in the church life we experience. Prayers improvised on the liturgical form of Judaism are a natural part of Paul's letter-writing style. His exhortations to prayer are addressed to the church in its common life and not just to the piety of individuals (cf. 1 Thess. 5.17, Eph. 6.18-19, etc.).

Although references to congregational prayer abound it is not possible to trace a common structure for the meetings of the various Christian communities such as had emerged in the second century. The Roman Catholic liturgical scholar, Anton Baumstark, in his book *Comparative Liturgy* has attempted to trace the main principles that govern the evolution of liturgical forms and texts. He sees a major movement from variety to uniformity notwithstanding adaptation to local need. The development of a common three-part structure of word/prayer/euchar-ist for Christian gatherings in the second century is an example of this.[1] The pattern probably emerged as the scattered Christian communities of the Roman empire became more aware of one another, a process that is already under way in the New Testament (Rom. 16.16, 1 Cor. 16.19 etc.). It allowed them to combine conveniently their responsibility to outsiders and their identity as God's new people. The very emergence of a common pattern pointed to their fellowship in the Spirit.

Synagogue Influence

It seems likely that a major influence on the prayer of the early church was a prayer of Judaism called *Tefillah* (Prayer) or *Shemonêh 'Esreh* (Eighteen Benedictions).[2] It was prayed at the morning, afternoon and evening services of the synagogue and was recited three times daily by pious Jews. Jesus' warnings against ostentation in prayer (Matt. 6.5; Mk. 12.40) are probably directed against the way this is done. The Instruction in the Didache (8.3) that Christians are to pray the Lord's Prayer three times a day probably reflects this Jewish practice. The prayer is also called *Amidah* (Standing) because during its recital the congregation stands. The first example of Christian public intercessory prayer that we have is a long and moving prayer at the end of Clement

[1] A. Baumstark *Comparative Liturgy* (Mowbrays, 1958) pp.15.19.
[2] Singer's *Authorized Daily Prayer Book* pp.46-56. For other versions see (ed.) J. J. Petuchowski and M. Brocke *The Lord's Prayer and Jewish Liturgy* (Burns and Oates, 1978).

of Rome's letter to the church of Corthinth (A.D. 96) and J. B. Lightfoot argues that the *Shemonêh 'Esreh* has strongly influenced this prayer.[1]

The *Shemonêh 'Esreh* is primarily a prayer of praise and thanksgiving but includes some corporate confession of sin and intercession. There is, for example, prayer for the sick, for the earth's fruitfulness, for exiles, elders and proselytes, and that God would remember and redeem Israel. The themes resemble those of Christian intercessory prayer. However it is noticeable that Christian prayer has a greater emphasis on petition. Non-Jewish concepts of prayer may be at work here but the main influence is Jesus' teaching on prayer as asking, seen for example in the Lord's Prayer.[2]

It seems that at this period texts were not fixed, but that those who prayed publicly improvised within an understood tradition and framework. The congregation shared in the prayer by their posture of standing and by repeated Amens.[3]

The Early Pattern

'We are a society with a common religious feeling, unity of discipline, a common bond of hope. We meet in gathering and congregation to approach God in prayer, massing our forces to surround him. This violence that we do him pleases God. We pray also for the Emperors, for their ministers and those in authority, for the security of the world, for peace on earth, for postponement of the end'.[4]

These words from Tertullian (A.D. 160-220) give something of the feel of early Christian intercessory prayer. It was the fervent urgent activity of a community who were receiving salvation from the one true God and who were committed to a life of goodness and love. From other ancient sources it is clear that these Christian assemblies were busy noisy affairs. They were presided over by a bishop and his presbyters, and deacons were responsible for the conduct of the meeting. The deacons not only gathered the people's gifts and handled relief for the community's poor, they directed the progress of the meeting, rebuked unruly behaviour, and called out instructions to the gathered company.[5] In smaller congregations it seems that seats were provided for most of the adults although children had to stand; in larger churches most would stand but benches were provided for the elderly and infirm.

After the homily had been preached up to four different categories of people would be singled out by the deacon; they would be called upon to pray, then the congregation would pray for them, and, after a final prayer by the bishop, the deacon would dismiss them.[6] These four

---

[1] J. B. Lightfoot *Apostolic Fathers* Vol. 1 part 1 pp.382-396.
[2] Baumstark *op. cit.* p.65.
[3] Oesterley, *op. cit.* p.71.
[4] Tertullian in J. Stevenson (ed.) *A New Eusebius* (S.P.C.K., 1957) p.174; cf. also p.172.
[5] *Didascalia* Ch. 12; Bingham *Antiquities of the Christian Church* Bk. 2, Ch. 20.
[6] Bingham *op. cit.* Bk. 14 ch.5.

categories were: the catechumens, who were under instruction in the faith; the energumens, who being possessed by evil spirits normally lived in their own part of the church and were cared for and prayed over by exorcists[1]; the candidates for baptism; and the penitents who were under discipline. After these had been dismissed the deacon or bishop would summon the people to pray and the liturgy of the faithful (prayer and eucharist) would begin. The form these prayers came to take seems to be preserved most fully in the Solemn Prayers that were recited on Good Friday in the Roman Liturgy.[2] The officiant announced a subject for prayer and the deacon told the congregation to kneel; after they had prayed for a while, the deacon called on them to stand, the officiant gathered the prayer together in a short prayer or collect. Then a new subject was given and the process repeated. In this way the Roman church prayed for the church, the bishop, the clergy and other orders, the laity, the Emperor, the catechumens, the needy, heretics, Jews and pagans. The topics of prayer were not the same everywhere and in Egypt (where the deacon announced the subjects) they included the due rising of the Nile, the city, the old, eunuchs, the safety of man and beast, backsliders, etc., etc. In this pattern the whole church was involved in the prayer; it was *the people* who prayed. As one ancient writer puts it, 'the presidents of the holy congregations . . . plead the cause of the human race before the divine clemency . . . joined by the sighs of the whole church.'[3]

The contrast with our experience of congregational intercessory prayer is considerable, not only in the way all were involved, but also in the way that ordinary life, the needs of Christians world wide, and the outworking of the church's ministry and mission, were prayed for.

Later Developments
The common prayers in the form just described soon disappeared from the church's public worship and it is only possible to sketch very briefly the subsequent history of intercession at communion. These later developments are not without their lessons for the church today and serve as the Holy Spirit's witness to the importance of intercession in public worship.

In the Eastern churches the prayers of the faithful were transformed by the loss of the priest's concluding prayer and the united prayers of the prostrate laity. The changes resulted in the litany form, consisting of the deacon's bidding and the people's response of *Kyrie eleison* ('Lord have mercy'). Although this diminished the people's part in the intercessions it had the merit of brevity in services that were becoming very long. Litanies proved popular and were introduced as a

[1] Bingham, *op. cit.* Bk. 14 ch. 5.
[2] G. Dix *op. cit. The Shape of the Liturgy* (Dacre/Black, 1945), p.42ff; see also G. G. Willis *Essays in Early Roman Liturgy* (Alcuin/S.P.C.K., 1964) ch. 1.
[3] Prosper of Aquitaine quoted in G. Wainwright *Doxology* (Epworth, 1980) p.225; Compare this description of Baptists praying in Russia; 'All stand; pastor leads in prayer. Noise like rustling of leaves all round, as each person prays his own prayer, the pastor's voice carrying over the rest.' (Giles Walter).

congregational devotion at other points in the service, so that gradually the structure of the eucharist came to be obscured and the original prayers of the faithful were overshadowed. Intercession in this new form continued to be important.

In both Eastern and Western churches the prayers of the faithful were also overshadowed by prayers of intercession in the eucharistic prayer itself. Scholars disagree about the origin of these prayers.[1] Some see them as originating in the custom of naming local individuals, living or recently died, in the eucharistic prayer. Others suggest that broader intercessions were part of the eucharistic prayers of Egypt from early days and were then adopted elsewhere. Either way these intercessions gained importance with the growth of the idea that prayer was more effective when associated with the eucharistic sacrifice. An important figure in this development was Cyril of Jerusalem (A.D. 349-386) who, for example, taught that 'we believe that these souls will obtain the greatest help if we make our prayers for them while the holy and most awesome sacrifice is being offered'.[2] Such teaching had the effect of diminishing the importance given to other intercessory prayer by the gathered church. Gradually the eucharistic prayer was whispered by the officiant out of a sense of awe and this opportunity for intercession was lost to the laity.

In the Western churches the extended prayers of the faithful described above were squeezed out because of the time they required and because the gradual embellishment of the liturgy decreased the time available.[3] Pope Gelasius (A.D. 492-6) limited the use of the Solemn Prayers to Holy Week and introduced a litany of the Greek type (called *Deprecatio Gelasii)* but this also in time dropped out of use. However in the ninth century intercession made a comeback with the introduction of the Bidding of the Bedes or Bidding prayer.[4] This was part of a vernacular devotion introduced after the sermon at mass on Sundays and Festivals. The term 'Bidding' derived from the Middle English word *bidden* (pray) as opposed to *beden* (command) and originally the priest announced a subject, the people responded with a *Paternoster,* and the priest added a collect before introducing a new subject. Gradually this was transformed into a long vernacular injunction to prayer recited by the priest to which the people responded with a *Paternoster.* Prayer for those who had recently died became expanded to prayer for all the faithful departed.

The Bidding Prayers exercised considerable influence at the Reformation and beyond. In many of the churches of the continental reformation they continued as biddings or as a direct intercession recited by the minister after the sermon. In England Henry VIII issued repeated orders controlling the style and subject matter of the Bidding prayers. The main effect of this was to substitute the king and his family

---

[1] G. Dix *op. cit.* pp.498-511; B. Spinks (ed.) *The Sacrifice of Praise,* pp.109-119.
[2] *Mystagogic Catecheses* 5.8.
[3] Baumstark *op. cit.* pp.23-4.
[4] F. E. Brightman (ed.) *The English Rite* p.1020ff.

as the first topic for prayer in place of the church and the pope, and then to lump together the clergy, Lords, and Commons, as a subsequent group. Archbishop Cranmer introduced a long prayer of intercession into the eucharistic prayer of the 1549 Prayer Book. This occurs at the same place as the short prayer of intercession for the living in the canon of the Roman Mass but probably owes much of its inspiration and wording to the Bidding Prayers.[1] In the Second Prayer Book of 1552 Cranmer transferred this whole section from the eucharistic prayer to become the prayer for the Church Militant that follows the offertory in the Book of Common Prayer.

Cranmer's other attempt to encourage intercession was the fine Litany that he first issued in 1544. Originally intended as one of a number of forms to be used in processions, in 1547 its use was changed to a prayer to be said by priest and people together kneeling in church before the beginning of the eucharist. As it became clear that the Reformation had failed to restore weekly communion the Litany was increasingly seen as a conclusion to Morning Prayer. The Litany had great strengths as a comprehensive and specific prayer of intercession in which all could be involved. However its strongly penitential tone and the great length and rigidity of Prayer Book Book morning worship worked against its use and acceptance in more recent times.

The later history of the Bidding Prayer is a further witness to the desire for intercessory prayer in worship. In the latter part of the sixteenth century preachers commonly recited the Bidding Prayer after announcing their text and added to it particular prayers for themselves and their hearers. Although the political conditions of the day led to the rigorous control of forms of public prayer the Bidding Prayer was never treated as a fixed formula. Canon 55 and 1604 laid down that the bedes be bidden 'in this form or to this effect'. Up to the middle of the eighteenth century many preachers substituted a long direct prayer of their own, despite controversy and attempts at control by the ecclesiastical authorities. This whole tradition points to a surprisingly strong commitment to the ideal of extempore petitionary prayer in public worship in the Church of England before the modern era.

[1] E. C. Whitaker *The Intercessions of the Prayer Book* p.40ff.

3. DARING TO PRAY

Comparing the lively references to prayer in the New Testament and the corporate exuberance of the practice of the Church of the early years with our own experience reveals that intercessory prayer today is in some disarray. Where public intercession exists at all it tends to be stilted, formal and shallow. Some of the causes of this are social.[1] The style of modern life does not give people the skills to contribute without embarassment at gatherings of the size of a local congregation. Television and printed matter exercise such an influence that few people are able to express themselves articulately in public and even fewer can do so in a way that includes their emotions. All this poses severe problems for those who lead worship today but the deepest roots of the poverty of intercessory prayer today are theological. The intercessory prayer of a Christian or a congregation quickly reveals their real working theology. The result today is hardly encouraging. Let us consider two typical examples, no doubt somewhat cruelly caricatured.

Picture a Rite A Parish Communion in a suburban congregation and imagine the biddings at the intercessions. There is unlikely to be an echo of the place of the following in the life of the congregation; gossip, mortgages, advertising, adultery, supermarkets, travel, diocesan quota, or evangelism. Sickness is defined in medical terms, mental anguish and death are probably out of sight. God's function is to bring peace and health in the personal and domestic sphere and to preserve the present social order if that turns out to be within his power.

Another example. Often at a prayer meeting someone will begin, 'Father, we just thank you that we are free to meet like this'. Such a prayer in no way takes hold of the way in which Jesus, the cross, and the Holy Spirit, make prayer possible. The word 'just' not only shows that the person stands within a definite tradition of prayer that he has made his own; it is also an expression of humility and of the distinctively modern embarassment in the face of mystery and emotion. The prayer shows how much the plight of Christians behind the iron curtain has captured the imagination of many English Christians—they are our heroes because as our suffering brothers they express something fundamental about what it is to be Jesus' church in a world alienated from God. But the prayer may also reveal a complete misreading of the Christian situation in England. It may interpret cultural diversity as hostility to the gospel and not be sensitive to aspirations toward good in modern culture; it may see God as absent from the world instead of active in it; it may indicate a flight from the responsibility and pain that are part of mission. Of course it may not; like most catch-phrases it can carry a number of meanings.

Intercessory prayer is undermined by a failure to grasp many aspects of the character and activity of God or to come to terms with the church's

[1] See Colin Buchanan, Trevor Lloyd, Harold Miller (eds.) *Anglican Worship Today* (Collins, 1980) pp.38-41.

situation in the modern world. This is not easily remedied; unreality in a church's prayer life requires careful, honest, even leisurely, appraisal before God by leaders and people. The twin need is to discover again what God is like and what he is doing in the humble and unpalatable present as opposed to some fairystyle past of church or nation. It means going beyond a superficial account of God's activity in the world and confronting modern doubts and half truths. What follows in the rest of this chapter is an introduction to four areas which leaders or groups could profitably explore for themselves.

1. A Philosophical bogey

Many suspect that intercessory prayer rests on an unworthy view of God and a pre-scientific view of nature and history. In response to such questioning the late Bishop Ian Ramsey produced a short booklet called *Our Understanding of Prayer*[1] which asks whether modern people 'can retain their intellectual integrity and still go on praying'.[2] It provides some very helpful insights into the language and logic of intercessory prayer and affirms that

> 'we hope for a responsive activity on the part of God which, not only inspires our own activity . . . but is also able to affect the universe in a particular way, and to bring about events which might not otherwise have happened.'[3]

Prayer, he says, must not be an attempt at human manipulation of God.

> 'Of course, we must have some idea of what we are asking God to do; but our prayers must not be *determined* by our supposed knowledge or ignorance of the particular cosmic machinery by which the results could be brought about. We must certainly not select out prayer concerns in a sort of superior way that presupposes that we ourselves are equal to God and have access to cosmic blueprints.'[4]

Jesus' teaching on prayer stands in stark contrast with ideas of a God who is excluded from the world he has made and whose majesty and being are compromised if he is ever seen to act or to attend to the concerns of men. Jesus speaks of prayer as *asking* (e.g. Matt. 6.8-14; 7.7-11; Mk. 11.24; John 15.16). Oliver O'Donovan writes,

> 'It would be difficult to exaggerate the extent of the tragedy that has come upon the church in the loss of this verb from its central position in the understanding of prayer, and its replacement by the idea of "communion", to which is often given a more or less prominent flavour of resignation and self-abandonment . . . At stake is nothing less than the Judaeo-Christian concept of God. Instead of a God who invites man into covenant-partnership, who establishes a relationship with him as between one agent and another (not *equal* agents, to be sure, but two free agents all the same); instead of a God who invites man to share his concerns, and who summons man to a real partnership of willing: instead of

---

[1] Archbishops' Commission on Christian Doctrine Occasional Paper No. 1 (S.P.C.K., 1971).
[2] *ibid.* p.7.
[3] *ibid.* p.21.
[4] *ibid.* p.17.

that God we are offered a deity whose will is absolute and determined, whose interest is not our human concerns but only in his own, before whom we can only resign all pretence at human will in self-abnegation'.[1]

2. God's activity in his world

'God bless Afghanistan.' 'Please be very close to Maud.' Much prayer seems to think of God as a sympathetic nanny rather than the just and loving Creator and Redeemer. If intercessory prayer is to get beyond banal generalities Christians must reach some understanding of the ways God is active in his world. Without this, prayer will lack of any definite content and will tend to lapse into thinly disguised sermons aimed at the congregation and not directed to God at all. Of course much of God's activity is hidden from us (Prov. 25.2; 19.21; 16.9). But the faith Christians are to exercise in prayer is not blind faith. It was while he was teaching about prayer that Jesus said, 'No longer do I call you servants, for the servant does not know what his master is doing; but I have called you friends' (Jn. 15.15). In discovering how God works and what to pray for Christians have their own experience of God's dealings with them to draw on and they have the promise of the Holy Spirit's guiding (Jn. 14.26; 16.23). However it is in scripture itself that we are shown most clearly the many different ways in which God acts in his world. The following list is not intended to be exhaustive but simply to provide some starting points from which people can think over how God is active in the world today. Select one or two, pray for the Spirit's enlightenment, and then try to explore modern implications of this facet of God's activity.

(a) *General:* James 4.6b, Ezek. 34.11, Acts 17.27-8, Rom. 4.5.
(b) *Nations:* Gen. 18.16-33, Is. 14.3-21, Jer. 18.7-10, Amos 1.3-12, Amos 9.7, Acts 17.26-27, Rom. 11.30-32, Eph. 2.11-15, Col. 3.11, Rev. 5.9-10. Rev. 11.15-19, Rev. 21.22-22.3.
(c) *Society:* Gen. 2.18, Ex.20.12-17, Deut. 10.17-19, Jer. 34.8-22, Amos 6.1-7, James 2.1-9; 5.1-11.
(d) *Communities:* Matt. 11.20-24, Lk. 19.28-44, Acts 18.1-10.
(e) *Economics:* Ex. 22.25-27, Deut. 15.1-11, Ps. 94.20, Amos 8.4-8, Matt. 6.25-33, Rev. 18.
(f) *Nature:* Ps. 65.9-13, Ps. 104, Deut. 22.6-7, Prov. 12.10, Matt. 6.26-29, Col. 1.15-17, Rev. 5.9-11.
(g) *Forgiveness:* 2 Chron. 33.1-13, Ezek. 18.21-32, Mk. 2.1-5(-12), Lk. 18.9-14; 23.32-43; 24.46-49, John 8.1-12.
(h) *Delight in man:* 2 Sam. 23.1-17, Prov. 8.15-31, Zech 8.3-12, Mk. 10.21, Lk. 2.40, 52.
(i) *Salvation/Kingdom:* Lk. 4.16-21; 8.43-48; 19.1-10, Acts 2.44-47, 3.16; 4.32-35, 1 Cor. 6.8, 1 Jn. 3.2.
(j) *Church:* Jn. 20.20-23, 1 Cor. 1.26-30, Acts 2.4-6; 3.8: 11.1-18: 13.1-3; 16.6-10.

---

[1] Unpublished communication.

3. The miracle of prayer

Christian prayer is not natural to us. We are finite, ignorant and confused. We know ourselves to be morally compromised so that we have no right to ask for the gifts of God's goodness and are not sure whether we want them anyway. We lack the energy to pray. Christian prayer is a miracle. It depends on God from start to finish and a church will not make progress in prayer until it understands why prayer is difficult and why it is possible. The three keys as to how prayer is possible are Jesus, the cross, and the Holy Spirit.

Christian prayer is prayer in Jesus. Jesus is both our brother and our saviour in prayer. Our prayer is possible because of Jesus' prayer during his earthly life, his prayer in Gethsemane, his prayer on the cross and his prayer for us now in heaven. At no point is the church alone in its prayer; at no point is Jesus out of his depth in our prayer. See Hebrews 2.17-18; 5.7-9; 7.23-27; Also Luke 3.21; 4.12; 6.12; 9.18; 9.28; 11.1; 22.31-32; 22.39-46; 23.32-46; Acts 2.32-33, 7.54-60.

Prayer rests on the fact of forgiveness and forgiveness flows from what Jesus achieved on the cross. It is from the cross that double-minded, morally compromised men and women gain the right to stand before God in prayer as his forgiven people. It is from here that the church receives the privilege, the responsbility and the freedom to pray for itself and for others. See Romans 5.1-11; Ephesians 2.4-14; 3.14-21.

Prayer requires energy and many of the problems of public prayer are not simply the problem of time, buildings, education and so on. Paul wrote to the Church at Rome, 'I appeal to you, brothers, by our Lord Jesus Christ and by the love of the Spirit strive together with me in your prayers to God on my behalf' (Rom. 15.30). Many of the apostle's exhortations to pray emphasize the place of the Spirit in prayer. In order to pray effectively the church needs not only insight from God but also the outpouring of divine energy, the gift of fervent and loving power to pray. The fact that prayer depends on the Spirit does not rule out the place of effort and struggle in prayer. Quite the opposite is true but the struggle will be ineffective and short-lived if it is not undergirded by a deep realization of the place in the Spirit in prayer. Alternative Intercession B in Rite A rightly begins, 'In the power of the Spirit and in union with Christ let us pray to the Father'. See also Ephesians 6.18; 1 Thessalonians 5.16-20; Romans 8; 12.11-12.

4. Political dimension of prayer

At first sight the Christians of the New Testament seem to be model citizens. St. Paul in a typical passage encourages them to live quietly, to mind their own affairs, to work with their own hands, to command the respect of outsiders and to be dependent on nobody (1 Thess. 4.11, 12). Yet they always seem to have been in trouble with the authorities. Thus in Thessalonica itself when the church was only three weeks old a mixed crowd of Jews and Gentiles hauled some of the leading Christians before the city authorities and accused them of 'saying there is another King, Jesus' (Acts 17.7).

Prayer is a political act. When a church prays it acknowledges an authority which the world around it does not recognize. Paul speaks of the churches as 'all those who in every place call on the name of our Lord Jesus Christ, both their Lord and ours' (1 Cor. 1.2). To pray is to look for help to a Lord who is not only above but also in a sense over against the bases of power in human society. Of course the church is not to seek confrontation (Rom. 12.18), but where a local church is not willing to stand apart from the community in some way and to make clear its prime dependence on God, its prayer will be undermined. This led to some very painful conflicts for the first Christians (cf. Heb. 10.32-34; Rev. 13.16-17). Where a church prays for God's salvation in some local situation and is willing to be used by him it may well find itself in conflict. Opposition may come from the local squire or council or from those whose lives are bound up with some social, cultural or economic aspect of local life.

When Peter healed the lame man at the Beautiful gate he and John found themselves on trial before the social, religious, political and intellectual establishment of their day (Acts 3-4). The healing was in answer to prayer (3.16) and was perceived as a political threat (4.7) from a group outside the structures of power (4.13). Conflict did not escalate because what God had done was recognized as good (4.14). and because God gave the church protection, courage and winsomeness in answer to further prayer (4.23ff.). If the church is to take prayer seriously it must be prepared for trouble and it must be willing to persevere.

4. PRAYING

The flexibility offered at the intercessions by Rite A opens up a bewildering range of options that pose a considerable challenge to leader and congregation alike. Obviously different forms will be suitable for different contexts. What is right for the early morning daily eucharist of a parish or college will be wrong for a Sunday communion attended mainly by families with little church background. What works in a congregation that shares a common culture and in which people know one another well will go down like a lead balloon in a more mixed and scattered church or at a crowded Mothering Sunday service. Disastrous mistakes are quite possible. The story is told of a church in a well-heeled area of Sheffield where members of the PCC badgered the vicar to allow extempore prayer in the main services. At last he agreed and at a service with some hundreds present he invited those who wished to lead the congregation in prayer to come to the microphone and do so. A young man stepped up and began to pray that God would heal a rash on his mother's knees which she had got through eating too many strawberries. The congregation burst out laughing, the vicar switched the microphone off, and the experiment was never mentioned again!

Assessing the situation

Assessing what is possible for a particular service or congregation is essential if disaster is to be avoided. One factor is the building itself. Size, layout and acoustics will all affect the atmosphere of the service and what sort of contribution the people can make to the prayers. Obviously these are important for the whole service and not just for the intercessions. A few people scattered round a barn of a building will find it difficult to feel united in prayer, although space can be used to express the presence and greatness of God. Particularly important if people are to contribute to the intercessions is audibility. If people are to pray or make biddings from the floor they must be able to be heard. If the building does not allow this to be done with microphones then either the idea of contributions from the floor must be abandoned or a way found for people to reach a microphone without fuss or embarrassment. A number of microphones round the building might make this possible. If an individual or group is leading the prayers they must be audible and thought should be given to where they should stand.

Another factor is the time available for the intercessions. In many services this will be not more than five to ten minutes. It may be possible to expand this occasionally by juggling with other parts of the service but care needs to be taken to use the time available well rather than try the patience of the congregation. Equally significant is the time available for preparation by those who lead the prayers. Some options will be much more time-consuming than others and realism can avoid underprepared worship.

Perhaps the most important factor is the size and type of congregation. In a small congregation it should be quite practical for many people to contribute; with a large regular congregation the difficulties are much greater. Equally important is the congregation's level of understanding and spirituality. Congregations also differ, of course, in homogeneity. Four types are worth identifying. In the first people share a similar level of understanding and perhaps know one another well (Type A). In the second a spiritually enthusiastic group exists alongside a silent, and perhaps long suffering, majority (Type B). The third type is really the coming together of a number of vital smaller fellowships (Type C). The fourth type is the weekly meeting of individuals many of whom do not meet in the week and have Christian roots in other groups (Type D). All except Type A may need help in recognizing the true character of their meeting and quite unrealistic expectations may exist amongst some members of groups.

To recognize the factors that limit a situation is not necessarily to accept them permanently. Christian leadership involves commitment to the possibility of growth and change. For example, the time a church is willing to give to intercessory prayer should grow with increased understanding and commitment.

Setting a pattern

The objective limitations just discussed will probably leave most congregations with more options than they can absorb and be at ease with. People need form if they are to function freely and without anxiety. If people are to use and contribute to a particular framework of public intercession they will need to have a very clear grasp of its structure and of how and when they can contribute. Probably a congregation would find it best to agree on two or three quite distinct ways of doing the intercessions and then stick to these, using whichever was appropriate in a particular case. Particularly in the case of congregation types B, C and D agreeing to some common forms would enable a sense of united prayer which might be quite difficult to achieve in any other way.

Section 21 of Rite A is likely to be one of the forms of intercession that a congregation will adopt. As it can be done in quite a number of different ways it would be wise to opt for one, or two at the most, for a given congregation. The precise way the subjects for intercession are divided up in this prayer is discussed in chapter 5. Decisions need to be made (and then followed consistently):

(i) whether the optional paragraphs are to be used.

(ii) whether the versicle and response is to come before or after the paragraph i.e. conclude the section or be followed by a prayer.

(iii) which sections are to be used and what subjects are appropriate to each one.

This form is conceived as a single prayer beginning 'Almighty God . . .' and winding up with the optional 'Rejoicing . . .' This means that insertions should be thought of as prayers ('we pray for', 'Strengthen') and not as biddings ('let us pray for') and the appropriate expressions used. If the paragraph 'Almighty God . . .' is not used it could then take the form: bidding—silent prayer—spoken prayer, and so on in something like the ancient model. This would take more time and care would have to be taken that it did not become all biddings.

Apart from the alternatives set out in Rite A (section 81), forms of intercessions from other churches could be adopted as one option. The *Book of Common Prayer* of the Anglican church in the USA (ECUSA) has some excellent ones. The Good Friday intercessions from the new Roman Catholic services could also be used or adapted.[1] Litanies are a very effective way of engaging a group in specific prayer once their use has been explained. Amongst many others, the litany in Appendix 2 of Series 2 could be adapted for use.

Another option is the use of a sung version of the usual versicle and response. A subject for prayer is introduced by the leader (or by a member of the congregation). There is a pause and then a cantor sings the versicle and the people respond.[2] The whole intercession is concluded by the president with a suitable prayer. This would probably work quite well in quite informal settings and any suggested setting is only a starter; a church could produce its own.

In choosing two or three agreed forms for a particular congregation it would be wise to have at least one that could also be used for festival services and occasions when many outsiders would be present.

Involving the community

(i) *Awareness*
Many congregations need to be helped to see that the intercessions are a distinct and important part of the service and they are the responsibility and privilege of the whole church. Teaching, simple explanations, discussion and good example all have a part to play in this. It was noted earlier[3] that for a variety of reasons most modern people do not have the skills to take part easily in a gathering the size of a local congregation (and conversely many clergy haven't a clue how to handle a crowd!). Part of the importance of home meetings springs from this; people are more confident in themselves and can gain confidence as Christians. However if the intercessions are to take off as the activity of the whole church people will need to be helped through their embarrassment and equally helped to rediscover some of the skills we have lost. The whole area needs to be handled sensitively and lightly. A little gentle instruction and explanation is not violation of privacy nor is it a sin against the Holy Spirit; it can avoid years of awkwardness, not to say agony. One of the functions of informal gatherings of a congregation (e.g. barn dances) is to help the recovery of these skills. Sitting or squatting in silence while other people talk does not help you feel involved. It is worth suggesting that people adopt a posture that expresses their involvement in the prayer—kneel,

[1] *Sunday Missal* (Collins, 1978) p.195.
[2] See settings on inside back cover.
[3] See page 10 above.

stand, hands open and slightly uplifted, sway etc. Also people need to be encouraged not to be afraid of grunts, murmurs, Amens, exclamations such as 'Lord have mercy', as a background accompaniment to spoken prayer. Such sounds are part of how a larger gathering works, as recordings from Parliament remind us. They are an important way in which mood, emotion, and consent, find expression. The worship of the ancient church was a much noisier affair than we realize. One fourth century pilgrim records that while the Bishop of Jerusalem preached 'the voices of praise . . . can be heard outside the church'.[1] The odd Amen and Hallelujah would do us no harm!

(ii) *Extempore prayer*
This often has a strange mystique about it not unrelated to the social factors mentioned above. Spontaneous prayer is not much stranger than spontaneous conversation. New Testament Christians seem to have viewed such prayer as a sign of the Spirit's presence in an individual and a source of encouragement to them.[2] It does not follow that such prayer needs to be long-winded, grammatical or original ('Abba'). Nor does it follow that people need no guidance and encouragement, particularly to start with ('say "Jesus is Lord" '). Such prayer is not too holy to touch or mention. Public intercession is an appropriate place for such prayer. In most cases it should be brief—a short bidding or a one-entence prayer— and should be related to the subject area currently being prayed for.

The leader's task requires great sensitivity and some light-hearted courage. He needs to make clear what conventions are being followed ('a simple bidding', 'no need to finish your prayer with "through Jesus Christ" as I will finish the whole prayer at the end'.) Gaffes will need to be handled kindly in public, and gently but perhaps definitely in private. The structure of the time of intercession may have to be made clear more than once and articulated during the prayer time. ('Now let's spend five minutes praying for Kenya.' Even, 'would two or three people please pray for . . .'). It is important to encourage the retiring and not to aim for more looseness than the context and congregation can take. Sticking to short prayers and biddings in a clear structure should eliminate the dominant few; if not have a word . . .! Asking one or two people privately to pray can help get things going. Beginners can be helped by suggesting they write something out to read it.

Congregations types B and D will require firmer structuring and clearer guidance on subject areas. With type C it may be important to make clear that the situation is different from the smaller groups. Where someone wishes to contribute some exhortation or 'word from the Lord' the leader will have to be positive and sensitive. It is important that the idea of intercession is not undermined and where a church feels it appropriate it might be better to institute a slot before or after the sermon. Such a slot might include comment on scripture or sermon, testimony, exhortation, or 'prophecy'; it would be seen as part of the church's sharing of the word and would allow the important place of intercession not to be overshadowed.

[1] Egeria *Diary of a Pilgrimage* ch. 47. See also references on pp.5-6 above.
[2] Rom. 8.15-16; 10.9, 1 Cor. 12.3, Gal. 4.6.

(iii) *Lay involvement*
The practice is already widespread of lay people leading the prayers
and there are many possible variations on this.[1] Individuals, families,
or parish groups, are asked to prepare the intercessions as a whole or
the different sections are divided between different people. The
minister asking different people to read out prayers he has written or
decided on is hardly the fullest possible expression of intercession as
the task of the whole church! It may, of course, be a good start and a
good way of involving new people.

A number of problems arise in this area. People need to be encouraged
to be brief and to use natural, concrete and relevant language. It is very
important that leaders understand the basic form they are using and
the way the subjects for intercession are divided. Attempts to include
other set prayers are usually a failure as they violate the overall
structure of the prayer; it can easily become a collect within a collect or
a ramble that is more meditation than petition. One variation that may
work is to take a phrase or a sentence from a well-known prayer and
use it in a *short* paragraph to conclude a section in place of one set in
Rite A section 21. Other issues that may need talking through are
sermons disguised as prayers, hobby-horses, and controversial
expressions of opinion that ignore the place of consent in public
prayer. Production problems can loom large; the prayers can be too
long or inaudible. No silences may be left for the congregation to make
the prayers their own. Leaders may lack confidence in presentation
through lack of practice.

A simple way of helping lay leaders of the intercessions is to prepare a sheet
which explains the structure of the service and the local agreed forms and
which gives some basic advice and tips on writing the prayers. Probably
much more satisfactory is to get together a group of those involved and run a
short course of, say, four or five sessions. Each session should be a mixture
of (a) rehearsal and comment by the group (b) explanation of service
structure and discussion, and (c) input or Bible study on wider issues and
discussion. Chapters 1, 3 and 5 might provide material for (c). Further ideas
on the method of such a group can be found in the African Roman Catholic
booklet *Leading the Community Service.*[2]

(iv) *Group planning*
Discussion so far has left open the question of how decisions are made
in the area—the important decisions of what a church should pray for
and how it should order its prayers. Formal responsibility for the service
lies with the eucharistic President (Rite A; Note 2) but in practice the
truth that worship is the activity of the whole church finds expression
in a whole variety of ways. Many parishes now have a worship sub-
committee of the PCC which is responsible for fostering and guiding a
congregation's worship. The general topic of the intercessions is

[1] Michael Perham *The Eucharist* (Alcuin, 1979) has a very helpful seven-page
appendix: 'Leading the intercessions—a Guide for the Laity.'
[2] No. 7 of the series *Training for Community Ministries* (Collins, 1976) Meetings, 3, 4,
18-21 contain particularly helpful material.

particularly well suited to being explored and developed in this way. There are really two sorts of issues that need resolving. Firstly there are the practical issues of what options to use and how to organize and stage the prayers. Secondly there are the deeper issues of the place of intercession in a particular church. Both sets of issues deserve careful discussion, indeed there is place for more leisured and exploratory discussion that will face up to some of the implications the subject could raise for the wider life of the church. The worship sub-committee of the PCC or a specially set up group would be a good way of facing these questions. At the practical level such a group could also be given responsibility for mounting the intercessions and for involving other members of the congregation in leading them. When setting up such a group it is important to take account of the type of congregation (see page 16). Types C and D would need carefully balanced groups; type A could raise radical issues quickly; type B could be explosive and futile unless very well run.

Breaking new ground
(i) *Notices* can be among the most boring parts of a church service— repetitive, uninspiring, uninformative and, just occasionally, unintentionally humorous. Duplicated news sheets made available to every member of the congregation can remedy most faults. A news sheet can also become a really useful means of intrachurch communication and can include a regular slot for prayer topics. If this is done the actual notices in the service can then major on important issues. Different members of the church can give out their notices personally. Done in this way they can provide material for prayer e.g. 'In a moment of quiet please pray for one of the meetings listed on page 2'. 'Now that we have heard from Albert (treasurer/bookstall manager), Bertram and Ethel will each lead us in a brief prayer about the crisis/book fair'. This time can be used for members of the church to share their concerns and activities before prayer (type A).

(ii) *Buzz groups,* in which small groups form for a short time to pray, can be very helpful where architecture allows, and may be one of the two or three forms a church adopts. If insensitively or too personally done they can be counter-productive (e.g. 'share a tragedy with your neighbour in 40 secs'). However they are a good way of praying about a topic in depth. Two examples: (a) a ten-minute report each month from a church's link missionary concluding with three topics for praise, three for prayer, then five minutes in groups; (b) each group given a piece of paper listing some sick people, an evangelistic meeting etc.

(iii) *Tapes/slides* etc can stimulate imagination in prayer. They can be used for initial information ('slides from our missionaries'). Quality visual material can accompany prayer to great effect e.g. a slide of children at school; 'we thank you, Father, for the vitality of children etc. etc.' Rule of thumb; not too much, of good quality, produced so that it aids prayer rather than substitutes for it.

(iv) *Reports* Some aspects of church or local life can be reported on and then prayed about, e.g., the Mothers' Union, the young unemployed. Perhaps particularly appropriate for congregation type C.

Part of the whole

The relation of the intercessions to the whole service can be developed in a number of ways. For example, the theme of the readings can be taken up and even, in a more informal context, be made the basis of open prayer. The great danger is that intercession will be lost as a distinct part of the worship. (It is to be regretted, for instance, that the intercessions are omitted when baptism takes place at communion.) If the prayers of penitence are used at the beginning of the eucharist the intercessions have more hope of standing in their own right. The transition to the eucharist can then seem quite abrupt and can be helped if the intercessions have a more weighty ending. Three possibilities are worth mentioning:

(i) After 'accept these prayers . . .' the president adds a concluding collect. Sections 10 to 14 on ASB p.106 are suitable

(ii) One of the two prayers of humble access (section 29,82)

(iii) The president says the paragraph 'Rejoicing in . . .' (Rite A Section 21) or Section 13 of the ASB Funeral service followed by 'Merciful Father . . .' etc.

Alternative paragraphs can be used, e.g.

'Bring us all to your heavenly city, to the joyful gathering of thousands of angels, to the assembly of your firstborn sons, to the spirits of just men (good people) made perfect, to Jesus the mediator of the new covenant and to the sprinkled blood that promises peace. Merciful Father, . . .'

'Hasten, O Lord, the day when men will come east and west, from north and south, and sit at table in your kingdom and we shall see your Son in his glory. Merciful Father . . .'

'Lord and all-just Judge, grant to us and to all who long for your appearing the garland (crown) of righteousness on the great day of your coming. Merciful Father, . . .'

'Fill our hunger (emptiness) with the food that lasts, the bread of God which comes down from heaven and gives life to the world, with Jesus your Son. Merciful Father . . .'

5. PRAYING FOR WHOM?

The three forms of intercession set out in Rite A divide the possible subject matter of intercession up in quite different ways. Section 21 derives from Series 3 and by implication divides the possible topics between five areas:

(i) the church

(ii) the nations, our own nation, all men in their various callings

(iii) the local community, our family and friends, particular persons

(iv) the sick, suffering and needy

(v) the remembrance of the departed.

This division is not without its problems as will emerge in the notes below but it is likely to remain popular because the form is in the main text of Rite A, because the division itself is fairly straightforward, and because the prayer is flexible and open. Also of the three alternatives this is the only one that gives space for mixing prayer with thanksgiving after the biblical pattern.[1]

In deciding for whom to pray the possibilities are immense and the leader must be guided by a number of considerations. The first is obviously the teaching and example of Jesus and scripture. The second is the capacity, situation and concerns of the particular congregation. As God's people they are called to share in the work of prayer in a way that springs from their particular relationship to the total human community and to the wider body of Christ. It is not a question of praying for 'all men' (1 Tim. 2.1) with the thoroughness and objectivity of a statistician. Discerning the scope of prayer is a question of love and of sensitivity to the Holy Spirit. It involves becoming alert to the particular relationships and responsibilities that a particular church should be developing. Part of this means making use of the various aids such as the media and cycles of prayer which can broaden or discipline the sense of brotherhood from which prayer springs. A church may well feel that a weekly general intercession does not enable it to do justice to its concerns. One way forward is to set up prayer groups to pray with greater thoroughness about particular areas. Another is to follow the policy hinted at in earlier sections of setting aside blocks of time at particular services to pray about particular areas at greater depth. These two policies can work together with the small group being given an occasional opportunity to draw the whole church into its prayers. The notes that follow are not intended to be exhaustive but to pick out particular issues.

(i) The world

It is probably legitimate to see the petitions of the Lord's Prayer summarized in the plea, 'your kingdom come.' This is much more than a request that God will help the church to grow and be good or that he will shore up the structures and institutions of society. It is a prayer for divine intervention that will bring radical, even traumatic, transformation. It will involve explicit acknowledgement of God ('hallowed be your name'), the meeting of human need ('daily bread'), reconciliation ('forgive as we forgive') and mercy and deliverance in human anguish

[1] Rite A section 20 'INTERCESSIONS *AND THANKSGIVINGS*' Also Phil. 1.3, 4.6, etc.

('lead us not . . . deliver . . .'). The very important passage in 1 Timothy (2.1-8; 4.10) that urges prayer for all men has a similarly drastic thrust; it breathes a respect for the breadth and ordinariness of human life but it looks unambiguously for radical salvation in Jesus Christ alone. This has important implications for the scope and nature of Christian prayer.

First of all, Christian prayer for the world is prayer that all men may come to know and acknowledge Jesus Christ. It is interesting that this note is almost entirely absent from the ASB; it gets no mention in section 21 and only a brief mention in the alternatives of section 1 and in one intercessory prayer in Rite B. Series 3 patronizingly puts those without faith in the section for the sick and needy. Early Christian prayer was different. For example Clement of Rome in his great intercession prays, 'Let all nations know that you are God alone, that Jesus Christ is your child, and that we are your people and the sheep of your pasture.' (The prayer of an insignificant group in the back streets of Rome!). This has implications not only for the way we pray for the world but also for the way we pray for the church. Much New Testament prayer focussed on the evangelism of the church and the safety, courage, and success of those involved (e.g. 2 Thess. 3.1-2; Eph. 6.18-19; 2 Cor. 1.11; Rom. 15.30; Acts 4.29; etc.).

Secondly, prayer for 'kings and all in high office' (1 Tim. 2.2), for the political structures of society, is not prayer that nothing will change. It is indeed motivated by a deep desire that the rhythms and quality of life of ordinary people will be preseved in peace and by a recognition of the part that rulers play in this.[1] But to pray 'your kingdom come' is to pray for change, to pray against as well as for the institutions of human society. To pray for judgment as well as peace. The New Testament church knew this well (cf. 1 Pet. 4.12-19; 4.7, 1 Cor. 7.29-31; Lk. 21.5-36). Disaster and industrial crisis may be answered prayer ('your kingdom come' 'lead us not . . .').

(ii) Brothers and sisters
Awareness of brotherhood should be a powerful guide to the people for whom to pray. This is true under each head. The world: the young, the unemployed, artists, social workers etc. The church: the persecuted, the tempted, the discouraged, the backsliding. Also under this head space should be made for those who serve the church; Sunday school teachers, old peoples' visitors, choir. The local community: the fete, public servants, 'thank you for the joy we've experienced over yesterday's match', those to be married, friends. The needy: the old, the sick, the dying. Much of the beauty of the old litanies of the Eastern church derives from this sense. We could learn too from the ancient church's praying for groups ('will the confirmation class please stand as we give thanks and pray'). With so many shut away in mental hospitals there is surely a responsibility for prayer for them.

---

[1] Secular rulers were not mentioned in the *Shemoneh 'Esreh* but Jews, like Christians, prayed for the civil power. Cf. Ezra 6.10, 1 Macc. 7.33 and in the Misnah, 'Pray for the peace of the ruling power, since but for fear of it men would have swallowed up each other alive' (Aboth iii.2).

(iii) Local community (Series 3 added this subject heading)
Much concentration in prayer on national and international issues is tinged with a modern idolatry of the state. J. Ellul writes, 'That the state is one of the sacred phenomena of this age is hard to dispute . . . The state is the ultimate value which gives everything its meaning.'[1] Prayer for the local community is one way a church can rid itself of the blindness that fascination with this particular idol brings. This is a good topic for a group to explore. Graham Dow's booklet *The local church's political responsibility*[2] would provide practical help in 'seeing' into an area. Another idea is to sit down with four representative members of the congregation and talk through an ordinary day in their lives in order to identify the main preoccupations and anxieties of the community; a policy of prayer could flow from this—specific prayer for some feature of group in the community. Once a month a member of the church involved in some aspect of local life could be interviewed prior to a time of prayer about this area. A member of the local social services could be invited to speak and the issues later taken up in prayer. General Synod special studies might also be a useful starting-point.

(iv) The Church
This includes Roman Catholics, Methodists etc., whatever diocesan and pan-Anglican prayer cycles say!

(v) The Sick
These are probably best prayed for by name in a special prayer group unless some urgent cause suggest otherwise. Death is not the end.

(vi) The Departed
These are 'remembered' as part of the truce in the Church of England concerning prayers for the dead. 'we remember before you N, M and thank you . . .' is a possible form. The litany in ASB expresses clearly the two categories of 'the faithful departed' (i.e. the Christian dead), 'those who have died in the peace of Christ, both those who have confessed the faith and those whose faith is known to you alone'. Praying for all men whatever they have done about God in this life is not really part of any Christian tradition.

(vii) Man and Nature
It is some indication of our alienation from nature and our sense that God is not active in his creation that there is no section that acknowledges man's dependence on the natural world. 'Give us today our daily bread.' The American Prayer Book is better here; for example, one of its forms has the words,

> 'Give us all a reverence for the earth as your own creation, that we may use its resources rightly and in the service of others and to your honour and glory.'

The ancient litanies were not wrong to pray 'that the Lord send rain on the place that needeth it.' _____

Final note: prayer is not an alternative to action. Jesus said the opposite of prayer is not work but despair (Lk. 18.1). Praying is dangerous and can cause trouble; it invites God to act and he may require that we act. _____

[1] J. Ellul *The New Demons* p.80
[2] Grove Pastoral Studies no. 2 (1980).